The Countess of Escarbagnas by Molière

LA COMTESSE D'ESCARBAGNAS

Translated by Charles Heron Wall

Jean-Baptiste Poquelin is better known to us by his stage name of Molière. He was born in Paris, to a prosperous well-to-do family on 15th January 1622.

In 1631, his father purchased from the court of Louis XIII the posts of "valet of the King's chamber and keeper of carpets and upholstery" which Molière assumed in 1641. The benefits included only three months' work per annum for which he was paid 300 livres and also provided a number of lucrative contracts.

However in June 1643, at 21, Molière abandoned this for his first love; a career on the stage. He partnered with the actress Madeleine Béjart, to found the Illustre Théâtre at a cost of 630 livres. Unfortunately despite their enthusiasm, effort and ambition the troupe went bankrupt in 1645.

Molière and Madeleine now began again and spent the next dozen years touring the provincial circuit. His journey back to the sacred land of Parisian theatres was slow but by 1658 he performed in front of the King at the Louvre.

From this point Molière both wrote and acted in a large number of productions that caused both outrage and applause. His many attacks on social conventions, the church, hypocrisy and other areas whilst also writing a large number of comedies, farces, tragicomedies, comédie-ballets are the stuff of legend.

'Tartuffe', 'The Misanthrope', 'The Miser' and 'The School for Wives' are but some of his classics.

His death was as dramatic as his life. Molière suffered from pulmonary tuberculosis. One evening he collapsed on stage in a fit of coughing and haemorrhaging while performing in the last play he'd written, in which, ironically, he was playing the hypochondriac Argan, in 'The Imaginary Invalid'.

Molière insisted on completing his performance.

Afterwards he collapsed again with another, larger haemorrhage and was taken home. Priests were sent for to administer the last rites. Two priests refused to visit. A third arrived too late. On 17th February 1673, Jean-Baptiste Poquelin, forever to be known as Molière, was pronounced dead in Paris. He was 51.

Index of Contents

THE COUNTESS OF ESCARBAGNAS (LA COMTESSE D'ESCARBAGNAS)

NOTES

'La Comtesse d'Escarbagnas' was acted before the Court at Saint-Germain-en-Laye, on December 2nd, 1671, and in the theatre of the Palais Royal on July 8, 1672. It was never printed during Molière's lifetime, but for the first time only in 1682.

DRAMATIS PERSONAE
THE COUNT, son to the COUNTESS.
THE VISCOUNT, in love with JULIA.
MR. THIBAUDIER, councillor, in love with the COUNTESS.
MR. HARPIN, receiver of taxes, also in love with the COUNTESS. MR.
BOBINET, tutor to the COUNT.
JEANNOT, servant to MR. THIBAUDIER.
CRIQUET, servant to the COUNTESS.
THE COUNTESS OF ESCARBAGNAS. JULIA, in love with the VISCOUNT.
ANDRÉE, maid to the COUNTESS.

SCENE: Angoulême.

JULIA, THE VISCOUNT.

VISCOUNT
What! you are here already?

JULIA
Yes, and you ought to be ashamed of yourself, Cléante; it is not right for a lover to be the last to come to the rendezvous.

VISCOUNT
I should have been here long ago if there were no importunate people in the world. I was stopped on my way by an old bore of rank, who asked me news of the court, merely to be able himself to detail to me the most absurd things that can well be imagined about it. You know that those great newsmongers are the curse of provincial towns, and that they have no greater anxiety than to spread, everywhere abroad all the tittle-tattle they pick up. This one showed me, to begin with, two large sheets of paper full to the very brim with the greatest imaginable amount of rubbish, which, he says, comes from the safest quarters. Then, as if it were a wonderful thing, he read full length and with great mystery all the stupid jokes in the Dutch Gazette, which he takes for gospel.[1] He thinks that France is being brought to ruin by the pen of that writer, whose fine wit, according to him, is sufficient to defeat armies. After that he raved about the ministry, spoke of all its faults, and I thought he would never have done. If one is to believe him, he knows the secrets of the cabinet better than those who compose it. The policy of the state is an open book to him, and no step is taken without his seeing through it. He shows you the secret machinations of all that takes place, whither the wisdom of our neighbours tends, and controls at his will and pleasure all the affairs of Europe. His knowledge of what goes on extends as far as Africa and Asia, and he is informed of all that; is discussed in the privy council of Prester John[2] and the Great Mogul.

JULIA
You make the best excuse you can, and so arrange it that it may pass off well and be easily received.

VISCOUNT
I assure you, dear Julia, that this is the real reason of my being late. But if I wanted to say anything gallant, I could tell you that the rendezvous to which you bring me here might well excuse the sluggishness of which you complain. To compel me to pay my addresses to the lady of this house is certainly reason enough for me to fear being here the first. I ought not to have to bear the misery of it, except when she whom it amuses is present. I avoid finding myself alone with that ridiculous countess with whom you shackle me. In short, as I come only for your sake, I have every reason to stay away until you are here.

JULIA

Oh! you will never lack the power of giving a bright colour to your faults. However, if you had come half an hour sooner, we should have enjoyed those few moments. For when I came, I found that the countess was out, and I have no doubt that she is gone all over the town to claim for herself the honour of the comedy you gave me under her name.

VISCOUNT

But, pray, when will you put an end to this, and make me buy less dearly the happiness of seeing you?

JULIA

When our parents agree, which I scarcely dare hope for. You know as well as I do that the dissensions which exist between our two families deprive us of the possibility of seeing each other anywhere else, and that neither my brothers nor my father are likely to approve of our engagement.

VISCOUNT

Yes; but why not profit better by the opportunity which their enmity gives us, and why oblige me to waste, under a ridiculous deception, the moments I pass near you?

JULIA

It is the better to hide our love; and, besides, to tell you the truth, this deception you speak of is to me a very amusing comedy, and I hardly think that the one you give me to-day will amuse me as much. Our Countess of Escarbagnas, with her perpetual infatuation for "quality," is as good a personage as can be put on the stage. The short journey she has made to Paris has brought her back to Angoulême more crazy than ever. The air of the court has given a new charm to her extravagance, and her folly grows and increases every day.

VISCOUNT

Yes; but you do not take into consideration that what amuses you drives me to despair; and that one cannot dissimulate long when one is under the sway of love as true as that which I feel for you. It is cruel to think, dear Julia, that this amusement of yours should deprive me of the few moments during which I could speak to you of my love, and last night I wrote on the subject some verses that I cannot help repeating to you, so true is it that the mania of reciting one's verses is inseparable from the title of a poet:

"Iris, too long thou keepst on torture's rack
One who obeys thy laws, yet whisp'ring chides
In that thou bidst me boast a joy I lack,
And hush the sorrow that my bosom hides.

Must thy dear eyes, to which I yield my arms,
From my sad sighs draw wanton pleasure still?
Is't not enough to suffer for thy charms
That I must grieve at thy capricious will?

This double martyrdom a pain affords
Too keen to bear at once; thy deeds, thy words,
Work on my wasting heart a cruel doom,

Love bids it burn; constraint its life doth chill.

If pity soften not thy wayward will,
Love, feigned and real, will lead me to the tomb."

JULIA
I see that you make yourself out much more ill-used than you need; but it is the way with you poets to tell falsehoods in cold blood, and to pretend that those you love are much more cruel than they are, in order to make them correspond to the fancies you may take into your heads. Yet, I should like you, if you will, to give me those verses in writing.

VISCOUNT
No, it is enough that I have repeated them to you, and I ought to stop there. A man may be foolish enough to make verses, but that is different from giving them to others.

JULIA
It is in vain for you to affect a false modesty; your wit is well known, and I do not see why you should hide what you write.

VISCOUNT
Ah! we must tread here with the greatest circumspection. It is a dangerous thing to set up for a wit. There is inherent to it a certain touch of absurdity which is catching, and we should be warned by the example of some of our friends.

JULIA
Nonsense, Cléante; I see that, in spite of all you say, you are longing to give me your verses; and I feel sure that you would be very unhappy if I pretended not to care for them.

VISCOUNT
I unhappy? Oh! dear no, I am not so much of a poet for you to think that I ... but here is the Countess of Escarbagnas; I'll go by this door, so as not to meet her, and will see that everything is got ready for the play I have promised you.

SCENE II

THE COUNTESS, JULIA; ANDRÉE and **CRIQUET** in the background.

COUNTESS
What, Madam, are you alone? Ah! what a shame! All alone! I thought my people had told me that the Viscount was here.

JULIA
It is true that he came, but it was sufficient for him to know that you were not at home; he would not stop after that.

COUNTESS
What! did he see you?

JULIA
Yes.

COUNTESS
And did he not stop to talk with you?

JULIA
No, Madam; he wished to show you how very much he is struck by your charms.

COUNTESS
Still, I shall call him to account for that. However much any one may be in love with me, I wish them to pay to our sex the homage that is due to it. I am not one of those unjust women who approve of the rudeness their lovers display towards other fair ones.

JULIA
You must in no way be surprised at his conduct. The love he has for you shows itself in all his actions, and prevents him from caring for anybody but you.

COUNTESS
I know that I can give rise to a strong passion; I have for that enough of beauty, youth, and rank, thank Heaven; but it is no reason why those who love me should not keep within the bounds of propriety towards others.

[Seeing **CRIQUET.**

What are you doing there, little page? is there not an ante-room for you to be in until you are called? It is a strange thing that in the provinces we cannot meet with a servant who knows his place! To whom do you think I am speaking? Why do you not move? Will you go outside, little knave that you are!

SCENE III

THE COUNTESS, JULIA, ANDRÉE.

COUNTESS
Come hither, girl.

ANDRÉE
What do you wish me to do, Ma'am?

COUNTESS
To take off my head-dress. Gently, you awkward girl: how roughly you touch my head with your heavy hands!

ANDRÉE
I do it as gently as I can, Ma'am.

COUNTESS

No doubt; but what you call gently is very rough treatment for my head. You have almost put my neck out of joint. Now, take also this muff; go and put it with the rest into the closet; don't leave anything about. Well! where is she going to now? What is the stupid girl doing?

ANDRÉE

I am going to take this into the closet, as you told me, Ma'am.

COUNTESS

Ah! heavens!
[To **JULIA**]
Pray, excuse her rudeness, Madam.
[To **ANDRÉE**]
I told you my closet, great ass; that is the place where I keep my dresses.

ANDRÉE

Please, Ma'am, is a cupboard called a closet at court?

COUNTESS

Yes, dunce; it is thus that a place where clothes are kept is called.

ANDRÉE

I will remember it, Ma'am, as well as the word furniture warehouse for your attic.

SCENE IV

THE COUNTESS, JULIA.

COUNTESS

What trouble it gives me to have to teach such simpletons.

JULIA

I think them very fortunate to be under your discipline, Madam.

COUNTESS

She is my nurse's daughter, whom I have made lady's-maid; the post is quite new to her, as yet.

JULIA

It shows a generous soul, Madam, and it is glorious thus to form people.

COUNTESS

Come, some seats, I say! Here, little page! little page! little page-boy! Truly, this is too bad not to have a page to give us chairs! My maids! my page! my page! my maids! Ho! somebody! I really think that they must be all dead, and that we shall have to find seats for ourselves.

THE COUNTESS, JULIA, ANDRÉE.

ANDRÉE
What is it you want, Ma'am?

COUNTESS
You do make people scream after you, you servants!

ANDRÉE
I was putting your muff and head-dress away in the cup ... in the closet, I mean.

COUNTESS
Call in that rascal of a page.

ANDRÉE
I say, Criquet!

COUNTESS
Cease that "Criquet" of yours, stupid, and call out "Page."

ANDRÉE
Page then, and not Criquet, come and speak to missis. I think he must be deaf. Criq ... Page! page!

THE COUNTESS, JULIA, ANDRÉE, CRIQUET.

CRIQUET
What is it you want?

COUNTESS
Where were you, you rascal?

CRIQUET
In the street, Ma'am.

COUNTESS
Why in the street?

CRIQUET
You told me to go outside.

COUNTESS

You are a rude little fellow, and you ought to know that outside among people of quality, means the ante-room. Andrée, mind you ask my equerry to flog this little rogue. He is an incorrigible little wretch.

ANDRÉE
Whom do you mean by your equerry, Ma'am? Is it Mr. Charles you call by that name?

COUNTESS
Be silent, impertinent girl! You can hardly open your month without making some rude remark.
[To **CRIQUET**]
Quick, some seats;
[to **ANDRÉE**]
—and you, light two wax candles in my silver candlesticks; it is getting late. What is it now? why do you look so scared?

ANDRÉE
Ma'am.

COUNTESS
Well—Ma'am—what is the matter?

ANDRÉE
It is that ...

COUNTESS
What?

ANDRÉE
I have no wax candles, but only dips.

COUNTESS
The simpleton! And where are the wax candles I bought a few days ago?

ANDRÉE
I have seen none since I have been here.

COUNTESS
Get out from my presence, rude girl. I will send you back to your home again. Bring me a glass of water.

SCENE VII

THE COUNTESS and **JULIA** [Making much ceremony before they sit down]

COUNTESS
Madam!

JULIA

Madam!

COUNTESS
Ah! Madam!

JULIA
Ah! Madam!

COUNTESS
Madam, I beg of you!

JULIA
Madam, I beg of you!

COUNTESS
Oh! Madam!

JULIA
Oh! Madam!

COUNTESS
Pray, Madam!

JULIA
Pray, Madam!

COUNTESS
Now really, Madam!

JULIA
Now really, Madam!

COUNTESS
I am in my own house, Madam! We are agreed as to that. Do you take me for a provincial, Madam?

JULIA
Oh! Heaven forbid, Madam!

SCENE VIII

THE COUNTESS, JULIA, ANDRÉE, who brings a glass of water, **CRIQUET.**

COUNTESS [To **ANDRÉE**]
Get along with you, you hussy. I drink with a salver. I tell you that you must go and fetch me a salver.

ANDRÉE

Criquet, what's a salver?

CRIQUET
A salver?

ANDRÉE
Yes.

CRIQUET
I don't know.

COUNTESS [To **ANDRÉE**]
Will you move, or will you not?

ANDRÉE
We don't either of us know what a salver is.

COUNTESS
Know, then, that it is a plate on which you put the glass.

SCENE IX

THE COUNTESS, JULIA.

COUNTESS
Long live Paris! It is only there that one is well waited upon; there a glance is enough.

SCENE X

THE COUNTESS, JULIA, ANDRÉE [who brings a glass of water, with a plate on the top of it], **CRIQUET**.

COUNTESS
Is that what I asked you for, dunderhead? It is under that you must put the plate.

ANDRÉE
That is easy to do.

[She breaks the glass in trying to put it on the plate.

COUNTESS
You stupid girl! You shall really pay for the glass; you shall, I promise you!

ANDRÉE
Very well, Ma'am, I will pay you for it.

COUNTESS

But did you ever see such an awkward loutish girl? such a ...

ANDRÉE

I say, Ma'am, if I am to pay for the glass, I won't be scolded into the bargain.

COUNTESS

Get out of my sight.

SCENE XI

THE COUNTESS, JULIA.

COUNTESS

Really, Madam, small towns are strange places. In them there is no respect of persons, and I have just been making a few calls at houses where they drove me almost to despair; so little regard did they pay to my rank.

JULIA

Where could you expect them to have learnt manners? They have never been to Paris.

COUNTESS

Still, they might learn, if they would only listen to one; but what I think too bad is that they will persist in saying that they know as much as I do—I who have spent two months in Paris, and have seen the whole court.

JULIA

What absurd people!

COUNTESS

They are unbearable in the impertinent equality with which they treat people. For, in short, there ought to be a certain subordination in things; and what puts me out of all patience is that a town upstart, whether with two days' gentility to boast of or with two hundred years', should have impudence enough to say that he is as much of a gentleman as my late husband, who lived in the country, kept a pack of hounds, and took the title of Count in all the deeds that he signed.

JULIA

They know better how to live in Paris, in those large hotels you must remember with such pleasure! That Hotel of Mouchy, Madam; that Hotel of Lyons, that Hotel of Holland, what charming places to live in![3]

COUNTESS

It is true that those places are very different from what we have here. You see there people of quality who do not hesitate to show you all the respect and consideration which you look for. One is not under the obligation of rising from one's seat, and if one wants to see a review or the great ballet of Psyche, your wishes are at once attended to.

JULIA
I should think, Madam, that during your stay in Paris you made many a conquest among the people of quality.

COUNTESS
You can readily believe, Madam, that of all the famous court gallants not one failed to come to my door and pay his respects to me. I keep in my casket some of the letters sent me, and can prove by them what offers I have refused. There is no need for me to tell you their names; you know what is meant by court gallants.

JULIA
I wonder, Madam, how, after all those great names, which I can easily guess, you can descend to Mr. Thibaudier, a councillor, and Mr. Harpin, a collector of taxes? The fall is great, I must say. For your viscount, although nothing but a country viscount, is still a viscount, and can take a journey to Paris if he has not been there already. But a councillor and a tax-gatherer are but poor lovers for a great countess like you.

COUNTESS
They are men whom one treats kindly in the country, in order to make use of when the need arises. They serve to fill up the gaps of gallantry, and to swell the ranks of one's lovers. It is a good thing not to leave a lover the sole master of one's heart, lest, for want of rivals, his love go to sleep through over-confidence.

JULIA
I confess, Madam, that no one can help profiting wonderfully by all you say. Your conversation is a school, to which I do not fail to come every day in order to learn something new.

SCENE XII

THE COUNTESS, JULIA, ANDRÉE, CRIQUET.

CRIQUET [To the **COUNTESS**]
Here is Jeannot, Mr. Thibaudier's man, who wants to see you, Ma'am.

COUNTESS
Ah! you little wretch, this is another of your stupidities. A well-bred lackey would have spoken in a whisper to the gentlewoman in attendance; the latter would have come to her mistress and have whispered in her ear: "Here is the footman of Mr. So-and-so, who wants to speak to you, Madam." To which the mistress would have answered, "Show him in."

SCENE XIII

THE COUNTESS, JULIA, ANDRÉE, CRIQUET, JEANNOT.

CRIQUET
Come along in, Jeannot.

COUNTESS
Another blunder.
[To **JEANNOT**]
What do you want, page? What have you there?

JEANNOT
It is Mr. Thibaudier, Ma'am, who wishes you good morning, and, before he comes, sends you some pears out of his garden, with this small note.

SCENE XIV

THE COUNTESS, CRIQUET, JEANNOT.

COUNTESS [Giving some money to **JEANNOT**]
Here, my boy; here is something for your trouble.

JEANNOT
Oh no, thank you, Ma'am.

COUNTESS
Take it, I say.

JEANNOT
My master told me not take anything from you Ma'am.

COUNTESS
Never mind, take it all the same.

JEANNOT
Excuse me, Ma'am.

CRIQUET
Take it, Jeannot. If you don't want it, you can give it me.

COUNTESS
Tell your master that I thank him.

CRIQUET [To **JEANNOT**, who is going]
Give it to me, Jeannot.

JEANNOT
Yes, you catch me.

CRIQUET
It was I who made you take it.

JEANNOT
I should have taken it without your help.

COUNTESS
What pleases me in this Mr. Thibaudier is that he knows how to behave with people of my quality, and that he is very respectful.

THE VISCOUNT, THE COUNTESS, JULIA, CRIQUET.

VISCOUNT
I come to tell you, Madam, that the theatricals will soon be ready, and that we can go into the hall in a quarter of an hour.

COUNTESS
Mind, I will have no crowd after me.
[To **CRIQUET**]
Tell the porter not to let anybody come in.

VISCOUNT
If so, Madam, I give up our theatricals. I could take no interest in them unless the spectators are numerous. Believe me, if you want to enjoy it thoroughly, tell your people to let the whole town in.

COUNTESS
Page, a seat.
[To the **VISCOUNT**, after he is seated]
You have come just in time to accept a self-sacrifice I am willing to make to you. Look, I have here a note from Mr. Thibaudier, who sends me some pears. I give you leave to read it aloud; I have not opened it yet.

VISCOUNT [After he has read the note to himself]
This note is written in the most fashionable style, Madam, and is worthy of all your attention.
[Reads aloud]
"Madam, I could not have made you the present I send you if my garden did not bring me more fruit than my love...."

COUNTESS
You see clearly by this that nothing has taken place between us.

VISCOUNT

"The pears are not quite ripe yet, but they will all the better match the hardness of your heart, the continued disdain of which promises me nothing soft and sweet. Allow me, Madam, without risking an enumeration of your charms, which would be endless, to conclude with begging you to consider that I am as good a Christian as the pears which I send you,[4] for I render good for evil; which is to say, to explain myself more plainly, that I present you with good Christian pears in return for the choke-pears which your cruelty makes me swallow every day. Your unworthy slave, THIBAUDIER."

Madam, this letter is worth keeping.

COUNTESS

There may be a few words in it that are not of the Academy, but I observe in it a certain respect which pleases me greatly.

JULIA

You are right, Madam, and even if the viscount were to take it amiss, I should love a man who would write so to me.

SCENE XVI

MR. THIBAUDIER, THE VISCOUNT, THE COUNTESS, JULIA, CRIQUET.

COUNTESS

Come here, Mr. Thibaudier; do not be afraid of coming in. Your note was well received, and so were your pears; and there is a lady here who takes your part against your rival.

MR. THIBAUDIER

I am much obliged to her, Madam, and if ever she has a lawsuit in our court, she may be sure that I shall not forget the honour she does me in making herself the advocate of my flame near your beauty.

JULIA

You have no need of an advocate, Sir, and your cause has justice on its side.

MR. THIBAUDIER

This, nevertheless. Madam, the right has need of help, and I have reason to apprehend the being supplanted by such a rival, and the beguiling of the lady by the rank of the viscount.

VISCOUNT

I had hopes before your note came, Sir, but now, I confess fears for my love.

MR. THIBAUDIER

Here are likewise a few little couplets which I have composed to your honour and glory, Madam.

VISCOUNT

Ah! I had no idea that Mr. Thibaudier was a poet; these few little couplets will be my ruin.

COUNTESS
He means two strophes.
[To **CRIQUET**]
Page, give a seat to Mr. Thibaudier.
[Aside to **CRIQUET**, who brings a chair]
A folding-chair, little animal![5] Mr. Thibaudier, sit down there, and read your strophes to us.

MR. THIBAUDIER [Reads]
"A person of quality
Is my fair dame;
She has got beauty,
Fierce is my flame;
Yet I must blame
Her pride and cruelty."

VISCOUNT
I am lost after that.

COUNTESS
The first line is excellent: "A person of quality."

JULIA
I think it is a little too long; but a liberty may be taken to express a noble thought.

COUNTESS [to **MR. THIBAUDIER**]
Let us have the other.

MR. THIBAUDIER [Reads]
"I know not if you doubt that my love be sincere,
Yet this I know, that my heart every moment
Longs to leave its sorry apartment
To visit yours, with fond respect and fear.
After all this, having my love in hand,
And my honour, of superfine brand,
You ought, in turn, I say,
Content to be a countess gay,
To cast that tigress' skin away,
Which hides your charms both night and day."

VISCOUNT
I am undone by Mr. Thibaudier.

COUNTESS
Do not make fun of it; for the verses are good although they are country verses.

VISCOUNT
I, Madam, make fun of it! Though he is my rival, I think his verses admirable. I do not call them, like you, two strophes merely; but two epigrams, as good as any of Martial's.

COUNTESS

What! Does Martial make verses? I thought he only made gloves.

MR. THIBAUDIER

It is not that Martial, Madam, but an author who lived thirty or forty years ago.[6]

VISCOUNT

Mr. Thibaudier has read the authors, as you see. But, Madam, we shall see if my comedy, with its interludes and dances, will counteract in your mind the progress which the two strophes have made.

COUNTESS

My son the Count must be one of the spectators, for he came this morning from my country-seat, with his tutor, whom I see here.

SCENE XVII

THE COUNTESS, JULIA, THE VISCOUNT, MR. THIBAUDIER, MR. BOBINET, CRIQUET.

COUNTESS

Mr. Bobinet, I say, Mr. Bobinet, come forward.

MR. BOBINET

I give the good evening to all this honourable company. What does Madam the Countess of Escarbagnas want of her humble servant Bobinet?

COUNTESS

At what time, Mr. Bobinet, did you leave Escarbagnas with the Count my son?

MR. BOBINET

At a quarter to nine, my lady, according to your orders.

COUNTESS

How are my two other sons, the Marquis and the Commander?

MR. BOBINET

They are, Heaven be thanked, in perfect health.

COUNTESS

Where is the Count?

MR. BOBINET

In your beautiful room, with a recess in it, Madam.

COUNTESS

What is he doing, Mr. Bobinet?

MR. BOBINET
Madam, he is composing an essay upon one of the epistles of Cicero, which I have just given him as a subject.

COUNTESS
Call him in, Mr. Bobinet.

MR. BOBINET
Be it according to your command, Madam.

[Exit.

SCENE XVIII

THE COUNTESS, JULIA, THE VISCOUNT, MR. THIBAUDIER.

MR. THIBAUDIER [To the **COUNTESS**]
That Mr. Bobinet, Madam, looks very wise, and I think that he is a man of esprit.

SCENE XIX

THE COUNTESS, JULIA, THE VISCOUNT, THE COUNT, MR. BOBINET, MR. THIBAUDIER.

MR. BOBINET
Come, my Lord, show what progress you make under the good precepts that are given you. Bow to the honourable company.

COUNTESS [Showing **JULIA**]
Come, Count, salute this lady; bow low to the viscount; salute the councillor.

MR. THIBAUDIER
I am delighted, Madam, that you should grant me the favour of embracing his lordship. One cannot love the trunk without loving the branches.

COUNTESS
Goodness gracious, Mr. Thibaudier, what a comparison to use!

JULIA
Really, Madam, his lordship the count has perfect manners.

VISCOUNT
This is a young gentleman who is thriving well.

JULIA
Who could have believed that your ladyship had so big a child.

COUNTESS
Alas! when he was born, I was so young that I still played with dolls.

JULIA
He is your brother and not your son.

COUNTESS
Be very careful of his education, Mr. Bobinet.

MR. BOBINET
I shall never, Madam, neglect anything towards the cultivation of the young plant which your goodness has entrusted to my care, and I will try to inculcate in him the seeds of all the virtues.

COUNTESS
Mr. Bobinet, just make him recite some choice piece from what you teach him.

MR. BOBINET
Will your lordship repeat your lesson of yesterday morning?

COUNTESS
Omne viro soli quod convenit esto virile,
Omne viri....

COUNTESS
Fie! Mr. Bobinet; what silly stuff is that you teach him?

MR. BOBINET
It is Latin, Madam, and the first rule of Jean Despautère.

COUNTESS
Truly, that Jean Despautère is an impudent fellow, and I beg you to teach my son more honest Latin than this is in future.

MR. BOBINET
If you will allow him to say it all through, Madam, the gloss will explain the meaning.

COUNTESS
There is no need; it explains itself sufficiently.

SCENE XX

THE COUNTESS, JULIA, THE VISCOUNT, MR THIBAUDIER, THE COUNT, MR. BOBINET, CRIQUET.

CRIQUET
The actors send me to tell you that they are ready.

COUNTESS
Let us take our seats.
[Showing **JULIA**]
Mr. Thibaudier, take this lady under your care.

[**CRIQUET** places all the chairs on one side of the stage. The **COUNTESS**, **JULIA**, and the **VISCOUNT** sit down, and **MR. THIBAUDIER** sits down at the **COUNTESS'S** feet.

VISCOUNT
It is important for you to observe that this comedy was made only to unite the different pieces of music and dancing which compose the entertainment, and that ...

COUNTESS
Ah! never mind, let us see it; we have enough good sense to understand things.

VISCOUNT
Begin then at once, and see that no troublesome intruder comes to disturb our pleasure.

[The violins begin an overture.

SCENE XXI

THE COUNTESS, JULIA, THE VISCOUNT, THE COUNT, MR. HARPIN, MR. THIBAUDIER, MR. BOBINET, CRIQUET.

MR. HARPIN
By George! This is fine, and I rejoice to see what I see.

COUNTESS
How! Mr. Receiver, what do you mean by this behaviour? Is it right to come and interrupt a comedy in that fashion?

MR. HARPIN
By Jove, Madam, I am delighted at this adventure, and it shows me what I ought to think of you, and what I ought to believe of the assurances you gave me of the gift of your heart, and likewise of all your oaths of fidelity.

COUNTESS
But, really, one should not come thus in the middle of a play and disturb an actor who is speaking.

MR. HARPIN
Hah! zounds, the real comedy here is the one you are playing, and I care little if I disturb you.

COUNTESS
Really, you do not know what you are saying.

MR. HARPIN
Yes, damn it, I know perfectly well; and ...

[**MR. BOBINET**, frightened, takes up the **COUNT**, and runs away; **CRIQUET** follows him.

COUNTESS
Fie, Sir! How wrong it is to swear in that fashion!

MR. HARPIN
Ah! 'sdeath! If there is anything bad here, it is not my swearing, but your actions; and it would be much better for you to swear by heaven and hell than to do what you do with the viscount.

VISCOUNT
I don't know, Sir, of what you have to complain; and if ...

MR. HARPIN [To the **VISCOUNT**]
I have nothing to say to you, Sir; you do right to push your fortune; that is quite natural; I see nothing strange in it, and I beg your pardon for interrupting your play. But neither can you find it strange that I complain of her proceedings; and we both have a right to do what we are doing.

VISCOUNT
I have nothing to say to that, and I do not know what cause of complaint you can have against her ladyship the Countess of Escarbagnas.

COUNTESS
When one suffers from jealousy, one does not give way to such outbursts, but one comes peaceably to complain to the person beloved.

MR. HARPIN
I complain peaceably!

COUNTESS
Yes; one does not come and shout on the stage what should be said in private.

MR. HARPIN
I came purposely to complain on the stage. 'Sdeath! it is the place that suits me best, and I should be glad if this were a real theatre so that I might expose you more publicly.

COUNTESS
Is there need for such an uproar because the viscount gives a play in my honour? Just look at Mr. Thibaudier, who loves me; he acts more respectfully than you do.

MR. HARPIN
Mr. Thibaudier does as he pleases; I don't know how far Mr. Thibaudier has got with you, but Mr. Thibaudier is no example for me. I don't like to pay the piper for other people to dance.

COUNTESS

But, Mr. Receiver, you don't consider what you are saying. Women of rank are not treated thus, and those who hear you might believe that something strange had taken place between us.

MR. HARPIN

Confound it all, Madam; let us cast aside all this foolery.

COUNTESS

What do you mean by foolery?

MR. HARPIN

I mean that I do not think it strange that you should yield to the viscount's merit; you are not the first woman in the world who plays such a part, and who has a receiver of taxes of whom the love and purse are betrayed for the first new comer who takes her fancy. But do not think it extraordinary that I do not care to be the dupe of an infidelity so common to coquettes of the period, and that I come before good company to say that I break with you, and that I, the receiver of taxes, will no more be taxed on your account.

COUNTESS

It is really wonderful how angry lovers have become the fashion! We see nothing else anywhere. Come, come, Mr. Receiver, cast aside your anger, and come and take a seat to see the play.

MR. HARPIN

I sit down? 'sdeath! not I!

[Showing **MR. THIBAUDIER.**

Look for a fool at your feet, my lady Countess; I give you up to my lord the viscount, and it is to him that I will send the letters I have received from you. My scene is ended, my part is played. Good night to all!

MR. THIBAUDIER

We shall meet somewhere else, and I will show you that I am a man of the sword as well as of the pen.

MR. HARPIN

Right, my good Mr. Thibaudier.

[Exit.

COUNTESS

Such insolence confounds me!

VISCOUNT

The jealous, Madam, are like those who lose their cause; they have leave to say anything. Let us listen to the play now.

SCENE XXII

THE COUNTESS, THE VISCOUNT, JULIA, MR. THIBAUDIER, JEANNOT.

JEANNOT [To the **VISCOUNT**]
Sir, here is a note which I have been asked to give to you immediately.

VISCOUNT [Reads]
"As you may have some measures to take, I send you notice at once that the quarrel between your family and that of Julia's has just been settled, and that the condition of this agreement is your marriage with Julia. Good night!"
[To **JULIA**]
Truly, Madam, our part is also played.

[The **VISCOUNT**, the **COUNTESS**, and **MR. THIBAUDIER**, all rise.

JULIA
Ah! Cléante, what happiness is this! Our love could scarcely hope for such a happy end.

COUNTESS
What is it you mean?

VISCOUNT
It means, Madam, that I marry Julia; and if you will believe me, in order to make the play complete at all points, you will marry Mr. Thibaudier, and give Andrée to his footman, whom he will make his valet-de-chambre.

COUNTESS
What! you deceive thus a person of my rank!

VISCOUNT
No offence to you, Madam, but plays require such things.

COUNTESS
Yes, Mr. Thibaudier, I will marry you to vex everybody.

MR. THIBAUDIER
You do me too much honour, Madam.

VISCOUNT
Allow us, Madam, in spite of our vexation, to see the end of the play.

FOOTNOTES:

[1] After the peace of Aix-la-Chapelle in 1668, this newspaper never ceased to attack Louis XIV. and the French nation. In 1672 Louis XIV. attempted the conquest of Holland.

[2] *The name given in the middle ages to a supposed Christian sovereign and priest (presbyter) in the interior of Asia.*

[3] *Instead of naming the hotels (= mansions) of the great noblemen, Julia names the hotels (= inns) of the time. She thus shows where the countess had studied the aristocracy.*

[4] *They were pears 'de bon chrétien.' 'Choke-pears' renders rather weakly the poires d'angoisse of Mr. Thibaudier.*

[5] *Compare 'Tartuffe,' act ii. scene iii.*

[6] *The Martial who did not write verses, sold perfumery, and was valet-de-chambre to the king's brother. Martial, the Roman epigrammatist, lived in the first century after Christ.*

Molière – A Short Biography

Jean-Baptiste Poquelin is better known to us by his stage name of Molière. He was born in Paris, to a prosperous well-to-do family, the son of Jean Poquelin and Marie Cressé, on 15th January 1622.

It is said that a maid, seeing him for the first time shrieked, "Le nez!", a reference to the infant's large nose. The name stuck as a family nickname from that time. At ten his mother died and his relationship with his father seems to have been lukewarm at best.

It is probable that his education started with studies in a Parisian elementary school. This was followed with his enrolment in the prestigious Jesuit Collège de Clermont, where he completed his studies in a strict academic environment but also first sampled life on the stage.

In 1631, his father purchased from the court of Louis XIII the posts of "valet de chambre ordinaire et tapissier du Roi" ("valet of the King's chamber and keeper of carpets and upholstery").

Molière assumed his father's posts in 1641. The benefits included only three months' work per annum for which he was paid 300 livres and also provided a number of lucrative contracts.

To increase the spectrum of his skills Molière also studied as a provincial lawyer around 1642, probably in Orléans, but it is not recorded if he ever qualified. Up to this date he had followed his father's plans for a career and they had served him well; he seemed destined for a career in office.

However, in June 1643, when he was 21, Molière abandoned this path for his first love; a career on the stage. He partnered with the actress Madeleine Béjart, to found the Illustre Théâtre at a cost of 630 livres.

Unfortunately, despite their enthusiasm, effort and ambition the troupe went bankrupt in 1645. Molière, now in charge, due to both his acting prowess and his legal training, had run up debts, mainly for the rent of the theatre, of 2000 livres. Molière was thrown into prison. Historians differ as to who paid the debts but after a 24-hour stint in jail Molière returned to the acting circuit.

It was at this time that he began to use the pseudonym Molière. It may also have been to spare his father the shame of having an actor in the family; a lowly profession for his status in society.

Molière and Madeleine now began with a new group of actors and spent the next dozen years touring the provincial circuit. The company slowly gained in success. Molière was also writing much of what they acted. Sadly only a few plays survive from this period among them 'The Bungler' and 'The Doctor in Love'. They represent though a distinct move away from the Italian improvisational Commedia dell'arte and highlight his use of mockery.

Armand, Prince of Conti, the governor of Languedoc, now also became his patron in return the company was named after him. Sadly for Molière the friendship later ended when Conti, having contracted syphilis from a courtesan, turned towards religion and joined Molière's enemies in the Parti des Dévots and the Compagnie de Saint Sacrement.

Molière's' journey back to the sacred land of Parisian theatres was slow. However by 1658 he performed in front of the King at the Louvre (then a theatre for hire) in Corneille's tragedy 'Nicomède' and in the farce 'Le Docteur Amoureux' (The Doctor in Love) with some success. He was awarded the title of Troupe de Monsieur (Monsieur being the honorific for the king's brother Philippe I, Duke of Orléans). With the help of Monsieur, his company was allowed to share the theatre in the large hall of the Petit-Bourbon with the famous Italian Commedia dell'arte company of Tiberio Fiorillo. The companies performed in the theatre on alternate nights.

The premiere of Molière's 'Les Précieuses Ridicules' (The Affected Young Ladies) took place at the Petit-Bourbon on 18th November 1659. It was the first of Molière's many attempts to satirize certain societal mannerisms and affectations then common in France. It won Molière the attention and the criticism of many, but alas not a large audience. He then asked Fiorillo to teach him the techniques of Commedia dell'arte. His 1660 play 'Sganarelle, ou Le Cocu imaginaire' (The Imaginary Cuckold) seems to be a tribute both to Commedia dell'arte and to his teacher.

Despite his own preference for tragedy, Molière became famous for these farces, which were generally in one act and performed after the tragedy. Some of these farces were only partly written and performed in the style of Commedia dell'arte with improvisation over a sketched out plot. He also wrote two comedies in verse, but these were less successful.

In 1660 the Petit-Bourbon was demolished to make way for the expansion of the Louvre. Molière's company decamped to the abandoned theatre in the Palais-Royal which was in the process of being refurbished. The company opened there on 20th January 1661. In order to please his patron, Monsieur, who was so enthralled with the arts that he was soon excluded from state affairs, Molière wrote and played 'Dom Garcie de Navarre ou Le Prince jaloux' (The Jealous Prince, 4th February 1661), a heroic comedy derived from a work of Cicognini's. Two other comedies of the same year were the successful 'L'École des maris' (The School for Husbands) and 'Les Fâcheux', (The Mad also known as The Bores) subtitled Comédie faite pour les divertissements du Roi (a comedy for the King's amusements) as it was performed during a series of parties that Nicolas Fouquet gave in honor of the king. These entertainments led to the arrest of Fouquet for wasting public money. He was sentenced to life imprisonment.

In parallel with 'Les Fâcheux', Molière introduced the comédies-ballets. These ballets were a transitional form of dance performance between the court ballets of Louis XIV and the art of professional theatre which was developing rapidly with the use of the proscenium stage. The comédies-ballets developed by chance when Molière was enlisted to mount both a play and a ballet in the honor of Louis XIV and found that he did not have a large enough cast to meet the needs of both. Cleverly Molière decided to combine the ballet and the play to achieve his goals. The gamble paid off handsomely. Molière was asked to produce twelve more comédies-ballets before his death. During these Molière collaborated with Pierre Beauchamp. Beauchamp codified the five balletic positions of the feet and arms and was partly responsible for the creation of the Beauchamp-Feuillet dance notation. He also collaborated with Jean-Baptiste Lully, a dancer, choreographer, and composer, whose reign at the Paris Opéra ran for fifteen years. Under Molière's command, ballet and opera became professional arts unto themselves. The comédies-ballets closely integrated dance with music and the action of the play and the style of continuity distinctly separated these performances from the court ballets of the time; additionally, the comédies-ballets demanded that both the dancers and the actors play an important role in advancing the story. Intriguingly Louis XIV played the part of an Egyptian in 'Le Mariage forcé' (1664) and also appeared as Neptune and Apollo in his retirement performance of 'Les Amants magnifiques' (1670).

On 20th February 1662 Molière married Armande Béjart, whom he believed to be the sister of Madeleine. The same year he premiered 'L'École des Femmes' (The School for Wives), widely regarded as a masterpiece. It poked fun at the limited education given to daughters of rich families and reflected on Molière's own marriage. It attracted a lot of outraged criticism and ignited the protest called the "Quarrel of L'École des femmes". Molière responded with two works: 'La Critique de "L'École des femmes"', in which he imagined the audience of the previous work attending it. It mocks them by presenting them at dinner after watching the play; it addresses all the criticism raised about the piece by presenting the critics' arguments and then dismissing them. This was the so-called Guerre comique (War of Comedy), in which the opposite side was taken by writers like Donneau de Visé, Edmé Boursault, and Montfleury.

But more serious opposition was brewing, focusing on Molière's politics and his personal life. Some in French high society protested against Molière's excessive realism and irreverence, which were causing some embarrassment. Despite this the King expressed support for him. Molière was granted a pension and the King agreed to be the godfather of Molière's first son.

Molière's friendship with Jean-Baptiste Lully influenced him towards writing his 'Le Mariage forcé' and 'La Princesse d'Élide', written for royal divertissements at the Palace of Versailles.

'Tartuffe, ou L'Imposteur' was also performed at Versailles, in 1664, and created the greatest scandal of Molière's artistic career. Its depiction of the hypocrisy of the dominant classes was taken as an outrage and violently contested. It also aroused the wrath of the Jansenists (a Catholic theological movement, that emphasized original sin, human depravity, the necessity of divine grace, and predestination). The play was banned.

Molière was always careful not to attack the monarchy in any way. He had won a position as one of the king's favourites and enjoyed his protection from the attacks of the court. When the King suggested that Molière suspend performances of 'Tartuffe', Molière complied and quickly wrote 'Dom Juan ou le Festin de Pierre' (Don Juan, or, The Stone Banquet) to replace it. The story is of an atheist who becomes a religious hypocrite and is punished by God. But this too fell foul and was quickly suspended. The King, still keen to protect Molière became the new official sponsor of Molière's troupe.

With music by Lully, Molière presented 'Love Doctor or Medical Love'. The work was given "par ordre du Roi" (by order of the King) and was received much more warmly than its predecessors.

In 1666, 'Le Misanthrope' was produced. Molière's masterpiece. Although brimming with moral content it was little appreciated at the time and a commercial flop, forcing Molière to immediately write 'The Doctor Despite Himself', a satire against the official sciences. This was a success despite a moral treatise by the Prince of Conti, criticizing the theater in general and Molière in particular.

After the Mélicerte and the Pastorale comique, he tried again to perform a revised 'Tartuffe' in 1667, this time with the name of Panulphe or L'Imposteur. As soon as the King left Paris for a tour, the play was banned. The King finally imposed respect for 'Tartuffe' some years later, when he gained more power over the clergy.

Molière, now ill, wrote at a slower pace. 'Le Sicilien ou L'Amour peintre' (The Sicilian, or Love the Painter) was written for festivities at the castle of Saint-Germain-en-Laye, and was followed in 1668 by 'Amphitryon'.

'George Dandin, ou Le mari confondu' (The Confounded Husband) was little appreciated, but success returned with 'L'Avare' (The Miser), now very well known.

With Lully he again used music for 'Monsieur de Pourceaugnac', for 'Les Amants magnifiques' (The Magnificent Lovers), and finally for 'Le Bourgeois gentilhomme' (The Middle-Class Gentleman), another of his masterpieces. The collaboration with Lully ended with a tragédie et ballet, 'Psyché', written in collaboration with Pierre Corneille and Philippe Quinault.

In 1672, Madeleine Béjart died. It was a heavy blow to Molière who was already in declining health himself. However, he continued to write and his plays were eagerly awaited and performed. 'Les Fourberies de Scapin' (The Impostures of Scapin), a farce and a comedy in five acts was successful. The following play, 'La Comtesse d'Escarbagnas' (The Countess of Escarbagnas), is thought of as a lesser works.

'Les Femmes savantes' (The Learned Ladies) of 1672 is accepted as another masterpieces. It was born from the termination of the legal use of music in theater, (Lully had patented the opera in France and taken the best singers for his own works), so Molière returned to his traditional genre. It was a great success.

Molière suffered from pulmonary tuberculosis. One of the most famous moments in Molière's life was his last: he collapsed on stage in a fit of coughing and haemorrhaging while performing in the last play he'd written, in which, ironically, he was playing the hypochondriac Argan, in 'The Imaginary Invalid'.

Molière insisted on completing his performance.

Afterwards he collapsed again with another, larger haemorrhage and was taken home. Priests were sent for to administer the last rites. Two priests refused to visit. A third arrived too late. On 17th February 1673, Jean-Baptiste Poquelin, forever to be known as Molière, was pronounced dead in Paris. He was 51.

Under French law at the time, actors were forbidden to be buried in sacred ground. Molière's widow asked the King if Molière could be granted a normal funeral at night. The King agreed.

In his life Molière divided opinion. He was adored by the court and Parisians but loathed and reviled by moralists and the Catholic Church.

In 1792 his remains were brought to the museum of French monuments. In 1817 they were transferred to Père Lachaise Cemetery in Paris, close to those of La Fontaine.

In his 14 years in Paris, Molière singlehandedly wrote 31 of the 85 plays performed on his stage. His immensely popular legacy includes comedies, farces, tragicomedies and comédie-ballets.

Molière – A Concise Bibliography

Le Médecin Volant (1645)—The Flying Doctor
La Jalousie du Barbouillé (1650)—The Jealousy of le Barbouillé
L'Étourdi, ou le Contre-Temps(1653)—The Scatterbrain or The Bungler
L'Étourdi ou les Contretemps (1655)—The Blunderer, or, the Counterplots
Le Dépit Amoureux (16 December 1656)—The Love-Tiff
Le Docteur Amoureux (1658), 1st play performed by Molière's troupe (now lost)—The Doctor in Love
Les Précieuses Ridicules (1659)—The Affected Young Ladies
Sganarelle ou Le Cocu Imaginaire (1660)— Sganarelle or, The Self-Deceived Husband aka The Imaginary Cuckold
Dom Garcie de Navarre ou Le Prince Jaloux (1661)—Don Garcia of Navarre or the Jealous Prince
L'École des Maris (1661)—The School for Husbands
Les Fâcheux (17 August 1661)—The Mad aka The Bores
L'École des Femmes (1662; adapted into The Amorous Flea, 1964)—The School for Wives
La Jalousie du Gros-René (1663)—The Jealousy of Gros-René
La Critique de l'école des Femmes (1663)—Critique of the School for Wives
L'Impromptu de Versailles (1663)—The Versailles Impromptu
Le Mariage Forcé (1664)—The Forced Marriage
Gros-René, Petit Enfant (1664; now lost)—Gros-René, Small Child
La Princesse d'Élide (1664)—The Princess of Elid
Tartuffe ou L'Imposteur (1664)—Tartuffe, or, the Impostor
Dom Juan ou Le Festin de Pierre (1665)—Don Juan, or, The Stone Banquet (aka The Stone Guest, The Feast with the Statue)
L'Amour médecin (1665)—Love Is the Doctor aka Medical Love
Le Misanthrope ou L'Atrabilaire Amoureux (1666)—The Misanthrope, or, the Cantankerous Lover
Le Médecin Malgré Lui (1666)—The Physican in Spite of Himself aka A Doctor Despite Himself
Mélicerte (1666)
Pastorale Comique (1667)—Comic Pastoral
Le Sicilien ou L'Amour Peintre (1667)—The Sicilian, or Love the Painter
Amphitryon (1668)
George Dandin ou Le Mari Confondu (1668)—George Dandin, or, the Abashed Husband
L'Avare ou L'École du Mensonge (1668)—The Miser, or, the School for Lies
Monsieur de Pourceaugnac (1669)

Les Amants Magnifiques (1670)—The Magnificent Lovers

Le Bourgeois Gentilhomme (1670)—The Middle-Class Gentleman aka The Shopkeeper Turned Gentleman

Psyché (1671)—Psyche

Les Fourberies de Scapin (1671)—The Impostures of Scapin

La Comtesse d'Escarbagnas (1671)—The Countess of Escarbagnas

Les Femmes Savantes (1672)—The Learned Ladies aka The Learned Women

Le Malade Imaginaire (1673)—The Imaginary Invalid